HEAVENLY WHISPERS
HOW GOD SPEAKS WITH US

OtengMontshiti

HEAVENLY WHISPERS

How God speaks with us

COPYRIGHT ©2019

CONTACT ADDRESS: OTENG MONTSHITI

P O BOX M1139

KANYE

BOTSWANA

E-MAIL ADDRESS: otengmontshiti@gmail.com

Contact number: (+267) 74 644 954

All rights reserved. No part of this publication may be reproduced or transmitted, in any form or by any means, without permission.

Table of contents

Acknowledgement-5

Introduction-6

Chapter 1

Through testimonies-8

Chapter 2

Through nature-12

Chapter 3

Through situations-16

Chapter 4

Through dreams and visions-23

Chapter 5

Through the voice of His spirit-27

Chapter 6

Through His word-31

Chapter 7

Through His servants- 34

Chapter 8

Through praise and worship-38

Chapter 9

Through miracles-41

Chapter 10

Through our consciousness-44

Acknowledgements

Writing a book is not an easy task. Therefore I would like to thank our lord Jesus Christ, my family especially my lovely wife who supported me.

Introduction

How God speaks to us

God is the creator of the universe. He is perceptive and understanding. To Him, day and night are the same. When he speaks, every opposition blows and the mountains melt like wax.

He is constantly speaking to us in every situation. As a believer, don't limit God because He can use anything in his creation to express His will. In this book, we will be talking about the various ways God speaks to us as His children.

Chapter 1

Through testimonies

Many children of God do not take testimony giving seriously. However, it is essential before God. Every time you give your testimony, you give honor and glory to God. Did you know it wins souls for Jesus Christ? The Bible says, 'wiser is he who wins souls.' If God has blessed you with a promotion at your workplace, employment opportunity, good health, success, and prosperity, don't sit on that testimony. When we recount our story with others we help them get to know what God is like and what He can do and that can save somebody on the verge of backsliding. In simple words, it encourages people.

One day, a certain brother was complaining about his situation. He had been unemployed for a record of five years! At that time, a certain sister gave her testimony about how the Lord had blessed her with a permanent and high paying job after ten unsuccessful years of searching and prayers. The brother described above's face gleamed; He went on saying he would wait for God's time. You note how God uses testimonies to encourage other brethren in the Lord.

Testimonies fling open new doors of promotion and favor. A man who knew this secret was David. When he met Goliath face to face, he started to testify about the goodness of the Lord in his life. That's to say, how the Lord gave him the strength to kill a lion, bear, and how he protected him in the wilderness. Imagine what happened, he killed Goliath with a sling, and people started to glorify the Lord of David.

Chapter 2

Through nature

The sun was rolling down behind the western skies, and I was traveling by bus from my local village to another one which was fifteen to eighteen kilometers apart. At that point, we approached a steep slope and signboard marked 'dangerous curves ahead' appeared. We couldn't see beyond the slope. Right then, something struck my mind, this is what I had ascertained;

"I must not rely on my limited strength but the unlimited power of God. In life, I can merely see what is visible before me, but beyond that, it is God's known mysteries." It was God ministering to me implementing his creation of nature.

In life, as human beings, we solely perceive what is happening presently, but the next minutes are in God's hands.

If you want to know if God exists or not, sit down under a

starry sky at night, you will see the moon and the heavenly stars moving according to the laws of nature. And nature is God's creation.

As you roll out of bed in the morning, draw the curtains open and observe the sun rising beautifully in the eastern horizons. And notice how it ascends along the cloudless sky. You will realize that a higher being controls these things. God's faith-filled words created heaven and earth. (Genesis 1: 1-3)

When huge pillows of murky clouds are riding on the wings of the wind, and suddenly the skies open up (rainfall), it is God who is behind all these marvelous things. If you look at them meditatively, you will be inspired to seek and appreciate the Lord even more.

Chapter 3

Through Situations

In the Kingdom of God, nothing happens by mistake. Everything that you go through serves a specific purpose only known to Him. Even if you are unemployed, sick, rejected, and the likes; these serve a particular purpose in your life. If you want to know why you are going through that dark chapter, ask God. He is faithful; He will give you the right answer.

When a door closes in your life, don't complain. Kneel and thank God. In the year 2012, one of the companies in my country employed me. Guess what happened a few months later, I resigned because of personal reasons. However, within a month, I had secured a scholarship (Marketing Management). You see how God can close one door and open a bigger one.

One day, a car passed me by at a bus stop in Lobatse. A few minutes later, I waved at a car that was rolling down the road from Lobatse to Gaborone and it halted. I scrambled inside and we pulled away from the bus stop. We drove for roughly five minutes after which we saw a tragic accident. I recognized the faces and the car; it was the car that passed me by at the bus stop. Everyone in it perished. May their soul rest in peace. You see how God can use situations to preserve us.

However, God can permit situations to come across our path to test our motives. We all pray but He knows that sometimes we want blessings to boast not to uplift other people's lives. This is because He is using us as a bridge between Him and the widows, widowers, orphans, the sick, rejected, prisoners, and the like.

Not all situations are permitted by God to strengthen or build us up. Some of them are coming from the Devil. That's why

However, God can permit situations to come across our path to test our motives. We all pray but He knows that sometimes we want blessings to boast not to uplift other people's lives. This is because He is using us as a bridge between Him and the widows, widowers, orphans, the sick, rejected, prisoners, and the like.

Not all situations are permitted by God to strengthen or build us up. Some of them are coming from the Devil. That's whyHowever, God can permit situations to come across our path to test our motives. We all pray but He knows that sometimes we want blessings to boast not to uplift other people's lives. This is because He is using us as a bridge between Him and the widows, widowers, orphans, the sick, rejected, prisoners, and the like.

Not all situations are permitted by God to strengthen or build us up. Some of them are coming from the Devil. That's why you should ask God in prayer, and he will reveal everything to you.

Chapter 4
Through Dreams and visions

God can use dreams and visions to communicate with you. He can manipulate them to aid you make the right decision in life. He can utilize them to reveal his will or desire concerning your life.

For example, he used a dream to reveal to Joseph that he would be influential in life, and many people would bow down to him. Ultimately, after many trials and tribulations, he indeed became the prime minister of Egypt.

Another example, God told Joseph in a dream to take Jesus and his wife to Egypt until a specified period because the child's life was in danger. He used a dream to warn him.

Matthew 1:20 But while he thought on these things, behold, the angel of the Lord appeared unto him in a dream, saying, Joseph, thou son of

David, fear not to take unto thee Mary thy wife: for that which is conceived in her is of the Holy Ghost. (KJV)

God is still speaking to us using them because the word of God says; He was the same yesterday, today, and forever. However, we must be careful because some of the dreams come from the Devil. When you wake up, you must cancel all the dreams of the Devil in the spirit; pray for those that come from God to manifest in the natural realm.

In Christianity, it is God's will to share dreams and visions. However, you mustn't share them with people who are full of jealousy like Joseph's brothers.

Chapter 5

Through the voice of his spirit

Another way that God uses to communicate with his children is through His Spirit. The moment you are born again, the Holy Spirit comes and dwells in your heart. His mandate is to lead you all to the truth. It is also known as "the small still voice." You will always hear

Him whispering in your spirit.

1Kings 19:12 And after the earthquake a fire; *but* the LORD *was* not in the fire: and after the fire a still small voice.(KJV)

The Holy Spirit and God are one. Therefore, He will never speak anything which contradicts the word of God. If somebody has wounded or hurt you and you hear I voice telling you to "go and revenge." It isn't the voice of the Holy Spirit.

He will tell you to forgive and forget.

One day, I met a certain married woman who told me that while she was in the church service, she saw a certain brother and a voice said to her that he was her real husband from God. I asked her to support her statement with the scriptures, but she could not. God will never say anything like that because marriage is a covenant; nobody can break it.

If the voice that is talking to you is from God, it will provide a sense of inner peace because Jesus Christ is the princess of peace (Isaiah 9: 6). He provides peace beyond human understanding. Any voice that fills your heart with fear is not God's voice.

Chapter 6

Through his word

God cannot do anything that opposes His word. As you read the word of God, meditate upon it and act upon it; He reveals His will and desires to you. If you want to know God's will concerning your life, the answer lies within His word. If you want to get out of unbearable situations, the answer is in the Bible. If you are sick, healing is in the scriptures. If you wish to prosper, it is in the word of God. If you want a financial breakthrough, the answer is in the scriptures.

Psalm 119:105 NUN. Thy word *is* a lamp unto my feet, and a light unto my path. (KJV)

For example, Jesus Christ discovered his divine assignment in the word of God. It is impossible to discover your divine task outside the scriptures. And remember everything outside the word of God is a lie.

As I have mentioned earlier, when God speaks through dreams and visions, He will never oppose His word. The word of God is the foundation of your relationship with Him. If your faith is weak, eat more of the word of God, and it will grow. And as you read the word of God, the more His voice becomes clearer.

Chapter 7

Through his servants

God can use other people to correct, encourage, and confirm what He has already revealed to you. After King David had eliminated another man so that he could wed his wife, God was very annoyed. He used His servant, Prophet Nathan, to relay His message to him. Subsequently, he was punished severely by God (2 Samuel 12:1-31). Another example; He used Prophet Daniel to interpret King Nebuchadnezzar's dream.

My first day in a church service, God used his servant to reveal the cause of my problems. He said, "Can I speak to you, sir?"

"Yes, the man of God," I answered with a nervous voice.

"You possess the spirit of stagnation and are with the wrong company," he said, looking straight into my eyes. From that moment, God bestowed me the grace to part ways with the wrong people and established a relationship with people who added value in my life. As result, my life has been moving from one level of glory to another.

However, God will never speak anything he hasn't revealed to you or what you don't know. If somebody prophesies to you and says you are rich and God has never shown that to you, then that prophecy has a question mark.

Chapter 8

Through praise and worship

One day, I was in a seemingly impossible situation. I was about to give up when I heard a song in my heart, saying, "God is able to do just what He said He could do...." Then, I started to meditate upon these words, and my heart told me, "You shouldn't give up because God will fulfill His promises concerning your life. Don't give up yet."

There are times when I sing along to a song on television or radio during the darkest chapters of my life; peace would settle in my heart propelling me into a deeper spiritual dimension. That's how God can use praise and worship to speak peace and comfort into your heart.

Another biblical example is when King Saul was troubled in the spirit; David would grab his harp and praise God.

Then, he would experience peace in his heart.

1Samuel 16:22 And Saul sent to Jesse, saying, Let David, I pray thee, stand before me; for he hath found favour in my sight.

1Samuel 16:23 And it came to pass, when the *evil* spirit from God was upon Saul, that David took an harp, and played with his hand: so Saul was refreshed, and was well, and the evil spirit departed from him.(KJV)

Chapter 9

Through miracles

One day, a certain man in a wheelchair came rolling down into the church during a church service. A certain man of God laid a hand upon him. Then, he leapt up on his feet and pushed the wheelchair away. Guess what happened, that man was born again instantly and many other people devoted their lives to Jesus Christ. They jumped up and down, glorifying God. One sister said, "If God can heal this man, I know my miracle is on the way."

One day, Peter and John healed a lame man and he went to the temple to worship God afterwards. All miracles speak to people's hearts to dedicate their lives to God (John9:38). They also show them He is concerned about their welfare. They must steer people to God, not to a particular individual.

After God had divided the red sea, the children of Israel went ahead, glorifying God. That's how He can manipulate miracles to speak to your spirit or faith. He can indeed use them to talk to your spirit to seek him the more.

Chapter 10

Through our consciousness

Another tool God uses to communicate with us is the conscience. It is a mechanism God has placed inside us that communicates to us to know what is "wrong or right."

We must obey our conscience at all times. If you undertake a particular action without the approval of the conscience, the results may be destructive. If your conscience agrees with you, God agrees with you.

However, when we allow negative things to occupy our hearts, slowly but surely, our sensitivity to the word of God would diminish. Never hold grudges or offences in your heart.

1Timothy 4:2 Speaking lies in hypocrisy; having their conscience seared with a hot iron; (KJV)

The end

www.ingramcontent.com/pod-product-compliance
Lightning Source LLC
Chambersburg PA
CBHW031218090426
42736CB00009B/977